HE CALLS ME MAMA

A JOURNEY TO MOTHERHOOD

JEENA 'CHAHAL' DHANKAR

BLUEROSE PUBLISHERS
India | U.K.

Copyright © Jeena "Chahal" Dhankar 2025

All rights reserved by author. No part of this publication may be reproduced, stored in a retrieval system or transmitted in any form or by any means, electronic, mechanical, photocopying, recording or otherwise, without the prior permission of the author. Although every precaution has been taken to verify the accuracy of the information contained herein, the publisher assumes no responsibility for any errors or omissions. No liability is assumed for damages that may result from the use of information contained within.

BlueRose Publishers takes no responsibility for any damages, losses, or liabilities that may arise from the use or misuse of the information, products, or services provided in this publication.

For permissions requests or inquiries regarding this publication, please contact:

BLUEROSE PUBLISHERS
www.BlueRoseONE.com
info@bluerosepublishers.com
+91 8882 898 898
+4407342408967

ISBN: 978-93-7018-879-2

Cover Design: Aman Sharma
Typesetting: Pooja Sharma

First Edition: May 2025

For inquiries, permissions, or collaborations,
contact: chahaljeenaa@gmail.com

To Tejas—my son, my sunrise.

Dedication

To my firstborn, my Tejas.
One day, you'll ask me-
Mama, what is love?
And I'll hand you this book—
because every word in it
is the answer.

Love is you, my son.
Always and forever—
you.

Acknowledgements

This book would not exist without the love that raised me, the support that held me, and the moments that inspired me.

To Aditya, my darling husband—your quiet strength, constant presence, and unconditional love have held me together on days I didn't even realize I was unraveling. You are my calm in the chaos, my co-dreamer, and the father our son looks up to with sparkling eyes. You make this journey sacred.

To both my mothers—my son's grandmothers. You don't just help me raise him, you raise the sky above him. I've seen your arms become shields, your hands become lullabies and your eyes soften into stars each time you hold him close. In your love, I've found grace. In your protection, I've found peace. He is lucky. So am I.

To Ashutosh, my brother-in-law—Tejas shines in your presence. The way you laugh together, the way you lift his mood like magic. Thank you for loving him so loudly, so freely, so completely. He may not have the words yet, but one day he will know—that his Chachu's love is one of the first, truest gifts he ever received.

To my brother, Pulkit—your love may not shout, but it is steady, rooted, and real. Tejas feels it. And so do I.

To my sister, Kiran—the most amazing maasi. Fierce, fun, forever present. Your love for Tejas wraps him in laughter and light.

To our fathers—who teach Tejas where strength begins.

To our grandparents—your love carries him across generations.

To Rekha aunty who has been all things at once— a mentor, a mother figure, a friend in need, and a quiet force of grace—thank you. Your wisdom guided me, your strength steadied me, and your presence reminded me what it means to lead with heart and live with purpose.

To Shikhar Bhaiya—always ready to cheer up your nephew. He feels your joy like a second heartbeat.

To Riya, my soul sister—you are the wind beneath my wings, always motivating me, always reminding me who I am. This book carries your love between the lines.

To Dr. Sheena, my sister from another mother—thank you for holding my hand through the unknown, for making me believe in my strength, and reminding me that birth is as much a triumph of the heart as it is of the body.

To the ones who sent flowers every Wednesday, those flowers weren't just blooms, they were breath. A reminder that I was seen, loved, and quietly cheered for. Thank you for being the strength behind my soft days. For sisterhood that feels like shelter, and a brother whose quiet protection has always stood tall behind me.

To Dr. Chetna, you were there from day one. From the moment I conceived, you lifted me, guided me, and made me feel safe in the most vulnerable chapter of my life. Thank you for helping me bring Tejas earth-side with courage and calm.

To my friends—who knew how important it was for me to give him birth, thank you for holding space for my dreams, my fears, and my becoming.

To Aaron ji—our first baby, our softest goodbye. You may no longer walk beside us, but you run through every memory. You taught us how deep love can go, and your absence still fills rooms.

To each of you—thank you for showing Tejas what love looks like, feels like, and lives like.

This book is for him.

But it's also for you.

Author's bio

Jeena 'Chahal' Dhankar is a writer, poet, and mother whose words bloom in the quiet spaces between lullabies and laundry. Her debut poetry collection, He Calls Me Mama, is a tender reflection of the wild, raw, and wondrous journey of motherhood.

An alumna of Panjab University, Chandigarh, Jeena began her professional journey with the National Commission for Women. Today, she serves as the Assistant Director at a very prestigious institution (WCTM, Gurugram). Alongside her academic work, Jeena continues to explore storytelling through poetry that resonates with women, parents, and anyone who has ever loved deeply.

When she's not writing, she's wrapped in the giggles of her son, dreaming new verses over cold coffee and warm cuddles. She lives in a joint family surrounded by love, chaos, and endless inspiration-anchored by her husband, Aditya, and lifted by the everyday magic of motherhood. Her writing doesn't follow form, it follows feeling-flowing freely from the quiet corners of her heart to the pages that now carry her voice into the world.

Author's note

I didn't set out to author a book. I set out to hold on—to the moments that moved too quickly, to the love that grew louder every day, to the little boy who called me Mama and unknowingly rewrote me. This book is a collection of those moments. Of wonder and worry, of spilled milk and silent prayers, of first words, first steps, and the thousand invisible ways a mother becomes. These poems are not just about him—they're about me too. The me I discovered in the middle of the night, with tired eyes and a full heart. The me who broke and bloomed with every heartbeat of my son.

He Calls Me Mama is my love letter to my son—and to every mother who knows the ache of letting go while holding on.

With all my heart,

Tejas's Mama

Prologue

The Motherhood Mirror: A Thousand Ways to Be Enough

Motherhood doesn't come with medals or manuals—just opinions, undone laundry, and the quiet courage to keep going anyway.

Before I was a Mama, I thought I had to get it all right.

Now I know—being there, even when undone, is its own kind of perfection.

In motherhood—as in most things in life—there will always be people who want you to know how much better they are at it than you. They come armed with milestone charts, ancient remedies, internet articles, and that infuriating phrase: "Oh, really? Well, when we had ours..."

Yes. We've met them.

They show up as early as the hospital—while you're still lying there, stitched, and starry-eyed, wondering if you'll ever feel like yourself again—or if your insides will fall out the next time you sneeze. Someone leans over, while your soul is still catching up to your body, and asks, "What's your birth plan?" Birth plan? I barely had a dinner plan!

And—— then the comparisons begin.

"They're not crawling yet?"

"Oh, ours were walking at ten months."

"Do you not do baby-led weaning?"

"We only ever did hand-mashed organic vegetables from heirloom farms and served them on reclaimed bamboo."

It's not always cruel. But it's often unkind. Sometimes, even the baby joins in. No offense to their gurgly innocence—but a poorly timed poop explosion mid-criticism really adds insult to maternal injury. Suddenly, your parenting feels like a public performance. Your child's milestones become everyone's business. Your instincts are questioned by strangers, and your confidence, dear mama, is left wondering— if, you're screwing up the only job that truly matters to you.

But here's what nobody tells you loud enough: There is no "better." There is just "different." There is just you—figuring it out on three hours of sleep and six tablespoons of cold coffee.

And somewhere among the judgmental whispers, there are women who don't want to one-up you—they want to lift you. They want to laugh with you about the day they left the house with no wipes, no bra, and a teething baby chewing through their last nerve. They want to cry with you in the cereal aisle, just because the tiny one needed goldfish cracker NOW.

They are the absolute tonic. The voices are worth listening to. The ones who will carry you through the wild, wonderful, wobbly ride of motherhood and remind you that you're doing a damn good job.

This book is for you—the mom rooting through her bag for wipes that don't exist. The one who isn't sure if the library books are due back or already lost forever. The one whose husband misses her— but the baby needs her more right now. The one who forgot sunscreen, or gloves, or their own name for a moment. The one who's holding it all together until she's not. Who's better than ever, until she cracks mid-toast. This book is for the mom who shows up— on every messy, magical, marvelous day. Welcome to motherhood—the highest highs, the lowest lows, and all the joy, guilt, laughter, exhaustion, and magic in between.

Let's tell the truth. Let's laugh about it. Let's hold each other up.

And let's remember—most of us are just doing our best.

Including you.

Contents

Chapter 1: Becoming Mama 1

Chapter 2: The Language of Giggles 19

Chapter 3: Held and Holding... 33

Chapter 4: Messy Floors, Full Hearts 43

Chapter 5: Tiny Lessons, Giant Truths 57

Chapter 6: Your Firsts Are My Forever 69

Chapter 7: The Mama Mirror 81

Chapter 8: When He Lets Go... 93

Chapter 9: Always Home 111

He chose me

I didn't find him—
he found me.
A whisper in the dark womb
of uncertainty,
he stirred—
and my universe answered.
Not all miracles are loud.
Some arrive wrapped in silence,
with a heartbeat
that changes everything.

The two pink lines

I didn't cry.
I stood still—
as if joy might shatter
if I moved too fast.
Hope sat gently
on my trembling palms.
I was a universe,
and he,
a star learning
to shine within me.

Becoming

They speak of birth
as the baby's beginning—
but I was born too.
In that room,
with fluorescent lights and
hands guiding life out of me,
I met myself
for the first time.
Mama.
The name I didn't know
I had been waiting for.

The waiting

Nine months is not a countdown—
it's an awakening.
A stretching of skin
And soul.
A thousand silent conversations
between me and the life
growing inside.
He hadn't arrived,
but he was already everywhere.

Belly full of wonder

Strangers touched my belly—
but they didn't know
they were brushing against
an entire world.
A boy who danced to my laughter,
paused for my sadness,
and swam in dreams
too sacred for words.
I was his shelter—
and he,
my secret magic.

What if

What if I'm not enough?
What if I break?
What if my love
isn't enough to hold him whole?
But then—
he kicked.
Just once.
And all my doubts
took a breath
and made room
for faith.

Before he knew me

I whispered to him—
long before he knew words.
Promised him light,
long before he saw day.
I loved him
when he was only a dream
with a heartbeat.
Before he ever said "Mama,"
I was already
his.

The shift

The world stayed the same—
cars moved, clocks ticked,
people passed each other in silence.
But inside me,
the axis tilted.
I was no longer
just a woman.
I was someone's beginning.

Carrying you

I carried you in my body—
and now,
in my arms.
But someday,
I'll carry you in my stories,
in my prayers,
in the quiet
between heartbeats.
This is only the beginning
of a lifelong
holding.

The first hello

They laid you on my chest—

warm,

wet,

wailing.

And I—

I fell apart

in the most beautiful way.

Everything I'd been

ended,

so I could be

everything you needed.

The cord is still there

You lived in me—
I grew as you grew.
Our heartbeats synchronized,
one ancient, one new.

Before I knew
if you were a he or she,
you knew the sound
and rhythm of me.

From the moment you existed,
I was never alone.
And even now—
your body its own—
I feel that thread
between us hum.

It isn't seen,
but it is strong.
It pulls us back
when the world pulls long.

It was cord once.

Now, it's love.

And it tugs me gently

with every "Mama" you whisper of.

You made me new

Before you,
I was a name.
Now,
I am a home.

You made me
cry louder,
laugh harder,
feel deeper.

You made me
doubt myself—
then believe in myself
even more.

You made me new.
Not better.
Not worse.
Just real.
Raw.
Alive.
And full
of you.

Heartbeat without a sound

Before you were mine,
before you were even known,
you were a whisper
in the dark hollow of me.

No kicks,
no shape,
no name.
Just
a pause in my breath
that didn't belong to me—
a stillness too full
to be empty.

You were
a heartbeat
without a sound.
And yet,
my whole world
leaned in
to listen.

I dreamt you in Decembers

Long before the test turned pink,
before the cravings and lullabies,
I dreamt of you.
In cold months,
curled under quilts,
I imagined a warmth
that had nothing to do with weather.

You had no face yet,
but your presence
pressed gently against my soul.
You were an ache
and a promise,
a name I hadn't said aloud
but already whispered in my sleep.

Chapter 2: The Language of Giggles

The smile that saved me

It was a day like many others—
toys everywhere, dishes stacked,
me unsure of everything.

And you,
out of nowhere,
smiled.

Not a little smirk,
but a full grin—
toothless, brilliant,
completely unaware
of how perfectly timed it was.

And suddenly,
I remembered what mattered.
I was still your universe,
even if I couldn't keep mine together.
That smile saved me.
Again.

The first laugh

It wasn't just a sound—
it was sunlight breaking
inside a storm.
A burst of joy
so pure,
it made my eyes water
and my soul hush.
He laughed—
and I knew
I'd never be the same.

Talk without words

Before "Mama,"
before "Hi,"
he spoke in gurgles and glances—
language written
on the walls of my heart.
He didn't need to say a thing.
I understood every blink,
every sigh,
every wriggle.
Love has always been fluent
in silence.

His gurgle, my grace

You didn't speak
but you saved me.
In the soft gurgle
that escaped your lips
mid-bath,
in the high-pitched squeal
after your nap—
there was grace.

Not the kind
they write in books.
The kind that lifts a weary woman
who doubts herself.
The kind that reminds her—
she is doing enough.

Your gurgle
was my sermon.
And I never missed a word.

Soundtrack of us

Our days are made of
babbles and belly giggles,
raspberries blown mid-diaper change,
and squeals that echo like music
in a tiny, toy-strewn world.
No song on earth
sounds sweeter
than his joy
falling into mine.

Giggling at nothing

He laughs at shadows,
ceiling fans,
and his own toes—
as if the world
is made of magic
only he can see.
And I—
I laugh too,
because maybe it is.
Maybe joy lives
where logic doesn't.

Kiss symphony

I cover his cheeks
with kisses,
until he squeals—
that squeaky,
sudden, unstoppable joy
that makes my heart
leap into my throat.
He doesn't know
he's music.
But oh, how he plays me.

Peekaboo philosophy

He disappears behind tiny hands,
then returns—delighted,
as if discovering
he exists
again and again.
Peekaboo:
proof that joy
can be reborn
a thousand times
in a single day.

Your laugh, my prayer

Each time he laughs,
I offer it up
like a quiet prayer.
Let the world be gentle,
let life be kind—
but if not,
let him always find
reasons
to laugh anyway.

The joy we built

I stack blocks,
he knocks them down.
I make silly faces,
he howls in delight.
Together,
we build joy
from nothing—
over and over again.
He reminds me:
laughter is the only architecture
that never crumbles.

The mirror game

He smiles—
I smile back.
He mimics,
gurgles,
tilts his head.
And I see it—
the unspoken truth:
he's learning
what love looks like
by watching my face.

Born together

He let out his first cry—
and I took my first breath
as someone new.
In that same moment,
I birthed him,
and he birthed me.
He into the world,
me into motherhood.
His giggle—
my rebirth
echoing through time.

When arms became home

I used to hold books,

bags,

coffee cups.

Now I hold

a universe—

breathing, babbling,

wrapped in cotton and dreams.

And somehow,

I don't miss

anything I let go of.

Rocking chair theology

In a chair that creaks
like an old hymn,
I rock him through cries
and lullabies.
We say nothing—
yet everything heals.
This chair knows my ache,
and his rhythm.
Some days,
it's the only church I need.

We became us

There was a moment—
quiet, unmarked,
between a feeding and a sigh,
when the shift happened.
Suddenly,
it wasn't me anymore.
It was us.
Two souls braided
by need, by love,
by something far older
than language.

Skin to skin

Your chest on mine—
bare, soft,
more real than any name I had before.
No one told me
that your breath
would teach mine
a new rhythm.
You weren't just held—
you were memorized
into my heartbeat.

Sleepless and sacred

3 a.m. is lonely—
unless you're holding a soul
who once lived inside you.
The world sleeps.
We sway.
He drinks,
I hum.
Exhaustion and wonder
hold hands
in the dark.

Mama magic

He cries.
Others panic.
But I just
hold him close.
Because my body
knows his music.
I am his map,
his anchor,
his calm.
To the world, I'm "mother."
To him,
I am magic.

I carried you

Beyond Tired
People ask,
"Don't the night feeds exhaust you?"
But how do I explain—
my arms may ache,
my eyes may blur,
but my soul?
It blooms.
These breastfeeds don't tire me—
they teach me
how infinite love can be.

All of me

I gave him
my sleep,
my body,
my time.
Not because I had to—
but because I wanted to.
Unconditionally,
without pause,
without pride.
That's the kind of love
he pulled out of me.

Held and holding

He nestles in,
fingers clutching my shirt
like a lifeline.
And in that moment,
there's no world,
no time,
no self.
Just us—
woven in a hush
only mothers understand.
I hold him now,
but he's the one
who's holding me.

Chapter 4: Messy Floors, Full Hearts

Toy-strewn temples

My living room
used to be clean.
Now it's cluttered with blocks,
rattles,
half-eaten biscuits—
a shrine to boyhood
and growing up too fast.
And I?
I kneel among the toys,
grateful for the chaos
he brings.

Laundry and lullabies

Burp cloths.
Onesies.
Tiny socks that vanish
like whispered dreams.
I fold mountains of laundry—
not with resentment,
but reverence.
Because each stained bib
means one more day
I got to love him.

The unmade bed

My bed is no longer perfect—
the sheets rumpled,
milk-stained,
creased by little feet.
But it holds
midnight feeds,
morning snuggles,
giggles tangled in blankets.
Who needs neatness
when love
lives in the folds?

Spaghetti on the walls

He painted with dinner again—
spaghetti on the walls,
peas in his curls,
milk on the floor.
And yet,
I couldn't be mad.
Because in the middle of the mess,
he looked up,
grinning like an artist
who just created joy.

Crumbs and crayons

My floor crunches
beneath my feet.
Crumbs from snacks,
crayons cracked in half.
A mess to most—
but to me,
it's evidence
that a boy is learning
to live
out loud.

Mirror smudges

Tiny fingerprints
smudge every mirror,
and yet—
I can't bring myself
to wipe them off.
Because they remind me:
he was here,
reaching,
wondering,
growing—
right before my eyes.

A home rewritten

Once, I bought things
that matched.
Now, nothing does—
except the laughter
echoing in every room.
My decor changed.
My priorities shifted.
My heart?
Expanded
to fit a little boy
who sees beauty
in every mess.

Bath time floods

The bathroom floor's a lake again—
towels drenched,
shampoo lids missing,
giggles echoing off tiles.
And I just sit there,
soaked in joy.
Because this isn't a mess—
it's a memory,
dripping with love.

Tantrums and tenderness

He screams
because his toast broke in half.
I breathe,
kneel,
hold space for his storm.
Because love isn't only lullabies—
it's staying calm
when nothing else is.
Even his tantrums
teach me patience
I never knew I had.

Fullness

The house is loud.
Dinner's late.
My hair's a mess.
And still—
my heart is impossibly full.
This isn't the life
I dreamed of.
It's louder, messier,
more beautiful
than I ever imagined.

Socks don't match, but we do

He is in one yellow sock,
one blue.
And I am in sweatpants
from yesterday.
And dreams I folded away
to pack his snacks.

But then—
He laughs at the mirror,
and I laugh with him.
And I remember:
we're not here to impress.
We're here to connect.

We don't have to match the world.
We just must match each other.

The Teacher in the Crib

He doesn't speak in words yet,
but he teaches me still—
to marvel at fans,
to find rhythm in the rain,
to pause for pigeons on the sill.
Wisdom wrapped
in chubby fingers
and wide-eyed wonder.

The art of now

He doesn't plan.

He doesn't rush.

He sits in the moment—

mouth full of banana,

watching the curtain dance.

And I learn,

slowly,

that joy lives here—

not in what's next.

Falling with grace

He falls—
so often.
But never with fear.
He stumbles, wobbles,
laughs, tries again.
And I wonder:
When did I stop
believing that failing
is still flying
in its own way?

His entire world

Tiny shoes by the door,
never where they should be—
but always where he's been.
Each scuff a story,
each crease a journey
told in babbles and boldness.
He doesn't speak much,
but his steps
say everything.

Mama's here

He falls.
Not far—
but enough for tears.
And with just one hug,
my arms rewrite the moment.
He learns that pain is real—
but comfort is stronger.
I whisper,
"Mama's here."
And the world feels
whole again.

The way he looks at me

He looks at me
like I know everything—
where the toy went,
why the wind sounds scary,
how to fix the world
with just a kiss.
And somehow,
in that gaze,
I find the strength
to try.

My lap, his world

One day, he'll run—
into streets, into dreams,
into places I can't follow.
But today,
he climbs into my lap,
places his head on my chest,
and breathes like
I'm the only safe place
he knows.
And I am.

Willing to be exhausted

Nights break me—
hour by hour.
But then he stirs,
searches,
finds me.
And suddenly,
my arms forget their ache.
Because I know—
my tired body
is the home
his little heart trusts.

What he teaches without words

He doesn't say,
"Thank you for the milk,"
or
"I love how you rock me."
But he teaches me
that love is quiet.
That showing up—
bleary-eyed, broken,
again and again—
is louder
than words could ever be.

My greatest teacher

I thought I'd be the one
teaching him.
But he—
with his sleep fights,
his mid-meal cuddles,
his wide-eyed trust—
he teaches me instead.
How to rest in the moment,
how to rise when I'm tired,
and how to love
without limits.

The last time

No bell rings.
No one warns you.
One day,
you'll rock him to sleep—
for the last time.
Change the last diaper,
breathe in that baby scent
one final time.
And you won't even know
it was the last.
So today,
I hold him
like time is listening.

Firsts etched in me

His first smile—
my heart burst wide.
His first crawl—
I forgot how to blink.
Every first,
tiny to the world,
was a galaxy
to me.
Because when he begins,
I become.

Forever in a spoonful

He opened his mouth,
and I fed him
one little bite of mashed banana.
He blinked,
chewed,
and smiled with his whole face.
And I stood there,
realizing—
this is forever.
Not the banana,
but the way he trusts me
to give
and give
and give.

The first wave

He waved today.
A wobbly, curious motion—
open palm,
wide grin,
as if saying
"Look, Mama, I'm part of the world now."
And though it lasted seconds,
that tiny wave
rippled through my forever.

When he sat up

He sat today—
without help,
without falling,
as if the earth had shifted
to support him.
His eyes sparkled
with pride.
Mine with tears.
Because he didn't just sit—
he rose
into a new chapter
of becoming.

First crawl

One moment—still.
The next—
motion.
Knees planted,
hands forward,
determination in every wobble.
He crawled—
and the floor became a map
of wonder.
I watched, breathless,
as my baby
moved away
just far enough
to break me
and build me
at once.

The smallest triumphs

No one clapped
when he turned his head to my voice,
or reached for the toy,
or giggled at the ceiling fan.
But I did.
Because I knew—
in the quiet world of firsts,
the smallest triumphs
are the ones
etched deepest.

First step

One foot,
then the other—
like the earth
was whispering,
"Go."
He let go of the couch,
then of my hand,
then of needing
anything but courage.
And I cheered through tears,
knowing
his journey
had just begun.

First mama

It wasn't just a word—

it was a sunrise.

Soft.

Sacred.

He looked at me,

eyes full of knowing,

and said it:

"Mama."

And in that breath,

my name became

my purpose.

I remember everything

The world says,
"You'll forget these days."
But I won't.
Not the weight of him
on my chest,
the way he fit
exactly right on my hip,
or the sound
of his sleepy sigh
against my neck.
His firsts may fade
for him—
but in me,
they live forever.

You were given this child

You—
not by chance,
not by mistake,
but by divine knowing.
You were given this child
because your soul
was crafted
to hold his storms
and soothe his skies.

You are his anchor
on the hard days,
his light
when the world feels loud.
Your arms are a refuge,
your voice, a home.

And when you question
if you are enough—
look into his eyes.
He already knows
you are.

His eyes don't lie

In the mirror,
I see messy hair,
tired eyes,
milk-stained clothes.
But in his eyes—
I am warmth.
I am wonder.
I am perfect.
He doesn't see flaws.
He sees **me**.
And I'm learning
to see me too.

Enough

On the days
I feel like I'm falling short,
he wraps his arms around my neck
like I've done everything right.
His love doesn't measure—
it believes.
And slowly,
I begin to believe,
too.

Becoming through him

Before him,
I knew strength
in pieces.
Since him,
I know it
in full.
He made me softer—
not weaker.
He made me louder—
not less graceful.
Through his eyes,
I met a version of myself
I didn't know I was waiting
to be seen.

My name is mama

I had names before—
friend, daughter, lover,
even dreamer.
But none wrapped around me
like **Mama** does.
It holds the ache,
the joy,
the breathless awe.
It's the name
I never asked for—
but now,
can't live without.

Forgiving myself

I forgot the pacifier.
I lost my temper.
I cried in the kitchen,
quietly,
so he wouldn't hear.
But later,
he reached for me
like nothing had changed.
And I realized—
in his love,
there is room
to forgive myself.

This body

Stretch marks.
Soft belly.
Heavy arms from carrying love.
This body doesn't look
like it used to.
But it made him.
Fed him.
Held him through every fear.
And when he lays his head
against my heart—
I know,
it is holy.

More than enough

He doesn't ask me
to be perfect.
Just present.
He doesn't count
how many things I do—
only how fully I do them.
In his world,
I am not failing.
I am the answer
to every question
he doesn't yet know how to ask.

Chosen again

Every time he cries
and reaches for me,
I am chosen—
again.
Not for being flawless,
but for being his.
It's not my perfection
he looks for—
it's my presence.
And that,
I can give
without end.

Mirror of love

I once searched for worth

in mirrors,

in praise,

in doing more.

Now,

I find it

in the way he clings to me,

laughs with me,

calls out for me

in sleep.

His love reflects back

the best version of me—

even on the days

I can't see it.

Chapter 8:
When He Lets Go

The first letting go

He toddled across the room—
not far,
but far enough
to make my arms ache.
He didn't look back.
And I smiled,
even as my heart whispered,
You can let go, Mama—
he'll always find his way back.

From arms to ankles

He used to live on my hip—
clinging, curled,
always close.
Now he slips away,
barefoot and bold,
chasing light across the floor.
And I watch,
half-proud,
half-broken,
entirely in love.

Just a few steps away

He doesn't need my hand
to walk anymore.
But he still checks—
mid-step, mid-giggle—
to make sure I'm watching.
And I am.
I always am.
Even as he moves away,
he carries
everything I've poured
into him.

The bed climb

He used to wait—
arms up,
eyes wide,
trusting I would lift him
to the clouds.
Now he tries to climb the bed himself,
determined,
grunting with effort,
bruising my heart
with pride.

The toy instead of me

He crawls into the corner
of the room,
chattering to a stuffed animal
instead of curling into my lap.
And I sit nearby,
watching him build his world
without me in the center.
A tiny letting go—
a giant ache,
wrapped in joy.

No more rocking

Once, he could only sleep
in the cradle of my arms.
Now,
he turns,
tucks in,
drifts off on his own.
I stay there a little longer,
not to watch—
but to remember
what it felt like
to be his moon.

When he pushes back

He pushes away the spoon.
He says "No"
without words.
He wants to do it
his way.
And I let him—
smiling, sighing,
learning to hold space
for the boy
who once lived
entirely inside my arms.

Still within reach

He runs toward the open door,
bare feet slapping the floor,
laugh echoing down the hall.
And though he leaves my arms—
he's still within reach.
Because love,
real love,
follows
without needing to hold.

The soft goodbye

Not all goodbyes are spoken.
Sometimes,
they're the moment
he chooses the swing
over my lap,
the floor
over my arms,
the world
over my chest.
And I let him go—
just a little—
because growing
requires space.

Always returning

He will let go—
of my finger,
of the habit of looking back,
of the need to be held.
But he'll return.
Not always to my arms,
but to my love.
Because what I've built in him—
patience, safety,
home—
will call him back
in ways
even he won't understand.

The distance in inches

He walks away now—
just five steps,
maybe seven.
But each one
feels like a mile.

He turns back quickly,
just to check—
Am I still here?
And I am.
I always am.

There's distance now,
but it's measured in inches.
My arms stretch easily.
My love doesn't have to.

He climbs me, then climbs down

He used to cling—
tight,
constant,
heavy as heartbeat.

Now he climbs me,
laughs,
and then—
climbs down.

It isn't rejection.
It's becoming.
It's confidence,
wrapped in baby skin
and biscuit crumbs.

And I let him.
Because I'd rather be
the soft place he leaves
than the hard place he fears.

The reach has changed

He still reaches—
but not just for me.
He reaches for the spoon,
for the light switch,
for the cupboard
I haven't child-proofed yet.

He is curious,
daring,
wobbly with wonder.

And while my arms ache
to hold him close,
my heart whispers,
"Let him reach.
Let him grow."
And then quietly,
"I'll always be the place
he reaches back to."

Closer than far

He runs to the edge
of the room,
laughing.
Feet unsure,
eyes sparkling.

I stay back,
just a few steps,
biting back the instinct
to follow.

He isn't far.
He's just a breath away.
And when he looks over—
I wave,
smile,
and let him believe
he's all alone.

That's the magic.
He thinks he's flying.
I know
I'm the wind beneath.

Not far, just facing forward

He doesn't want to be held
all the time anymore.
But he still wants me nearby.
He toddles ahead,
his back to me—
but every few steps,
he turns,
eyes bright with questions.

And when he sees me—
he doesn't stop.
He just smiles,
like that's all he needed
to keep going.

He's my everything

He's
the quiet in my storm,
the giggle in my silence,
the tiny hand that holds my world.

He's the dream I never dared to dream,
the hope I didn't know I needed,
the miracle wrapped in a smile
that greets my every morning.

He teaches me patience with a glance,
courage with every fall,
and love—raw, wild, and unfiltered—
with every heartbeat.

He's not just my son—
he's my becoming,
my forever,
my everything.

My heart has feet

He walks now,
but it's my heart
doing the moving.
Across rooms,
into the world,
further each day.
And though he drifts,
explores,
forgets to look back—
my love walks with him,
tethered by every kiss
he didn't know he was keeping.

I am his safe place

One day, he won't fit in my lap.
One day, he won't call me
just to say "Mama."
But I'll still be his safe place—
the memory he runs to
when the world is too loud,
too sharp,
too much.
Because I was the beginning.
And beginnings
never fade.

I am the constant

He may not always want
my arms around him.
He may grow curious,
defiant,
independent.

But I—
I will be the constant.
The one who always waits,
always watches,
always believes.

He is my miracle.
I am his anchor.
And anchors
don't drift.

He won't remember

He won't remember
how I held him for hours,
how I sang the same song
sixteen times,
or how I whispered prayers
into his fevered skin.
But I will.
And that's enough—
to have been his shelter,
even if only
in the beginning.

He doesn't know yet

He doesn't know
I hold back tears
when he sleeps
a little longer without me.

He doesn't know
I peek through doors
just to see
he's still breathing
peacefully.

He doesn't know
that I've memorized
every freckle,
every breath.

But one day,
he will feel
how deeply
he was loved.

My love outgrows nothing

He'll outgrow onesies,

and cartoons,

and holding my finger to walk.

But my love?

It outgrows nothing.

It stretches with him,

follows every version of him

he'll become.

No matter his size,

his silence,

his distance—

he'll never outgrow

me.

The things I fold away

I fold his clothes
with slow hands—
not because I'm tired,
but because
I know one day
I won't be folding
this small.

I put away his bottle
knowing
the sippy cup
will soon follow.

I tuck away his blanket
like it's an heirloom.
Because in this house,
the smallest things
carry the loudest love.

The sound of his name

I say his name
like a hymn—
soft, steady, sacred.
It's in my breath
when I stir coffee,
in my thoughts
before I sleep.
He doesn't know
that even when he's far—
his name
echoes in my chest
like home.

The door will always open

He'll slam doors one day.

He'll leave,

for hours,

for years,

for things I won't understand.

But the door to me

will always open—

quietly,

without condition,

without pride.

Because love like this

asks nothing

but to be found again.

I'll still be there

He'll forget how he once
fit on my chest,
how my hum
was his lullaby.
But years from now,
when he's lost or lonely,
a familiar calm will rise—
and he won't know it,
but it will be me,
still there,
loving him
quietly.

My love doesn't expire

I won't always hold him
through his tantrums.
One day,
he'll handle the storm himself.

But even then—
my love won't fade.
It won't expire
with age,
or distance,
or silence.

It will live
in the way I answer the phone.
In the way I remember
his favorite shirt.
In the way
he never has to ask
if I'm proud.

My body remembers

His first cry.
His sleepy weight.
His hand wrapped around my finger.
Even when he's taller than me,
sharper with words,
quieter with love—
my body will remember.
The ache, the bloom,
the becoming.
Because motherhood
never forgets.

Home

He will travel
cities, dreams,
heartbreaks, triumphs.
He will find homes
in places I've never seen.
But a part of him—
the softest, oldest part—
will always know the way back
to me.
Because I was his first home.
And first homes
never fade.

He was my first forever

Before him,
love was fleeting—
a moment,
a phase,
a season.

But he—
he made love
eternal.

He made it stretch
into the future,
curl through memory,
settle into bone.

He was the first
to show me
what it means
to be forever
for someone else.

A note to my Husband

To the dad

We don't talk enough about what dads go through
after the baby arrives.

The sleepless nights you never post about.
The diapers you change
without anyone clapping.
The 6 a.m. alarms,
the long drives to work
after long nights holding our son.

You don't get a break.
You don't get a parade.
You don't even get space to say,
"This is hard."

But still—
you show up.

You see me break down,
and wish you could do more,
even as you're already doing everything
to keep this family afloat.

You hold steady
when I wobble.
You stay silent
when the world should be cheering you on.

Your love is quiet.
Consistent.
Unshakable.

You don't ask for credit—
but here it is.

Tejas and I,
we see you.
We feel your presence
in the calm you bring,
the pressure you carry,
the patience you live.

And I need you to know—
every act of yours
that goes unnoticed by the world
is etched into our every day.

To the dad—
the man who holds the fort
so I can hold our baby,
the one who wakes, works,
and still comes home with love left to give—

we appreciate you.
We love you.
And we know
none of this
works without you.

A note to my son

One day, you'll outgrow my lap.
You'll chase dreams I won't understand,
ask questions I won't know the answers to,
and walk paths I can only pray over.

But no matter how tall you grow,
how far you roam,
this truth will always hold:
You are my beginning,
my miracle,
my reason.

This book was written with your giggles in my ears,
your tiny hands tugging at my sleeve,
and your name folded between every line.

When life feels loud,
when the world forgets your softness—
read these pages again.
They'll remind you who you are.
And where you'll always belong.

Forever,
Mama

www.ingramcontent.com/pod-product-compliance
Lightning Source LLC
LaVergne TN
LVHW041607070526
838199LV00052B/3029